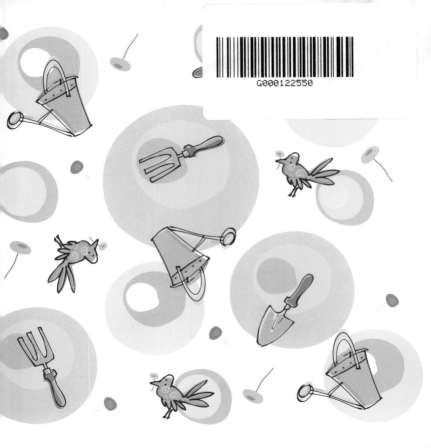

G000122550

Gardening forever, housework whenever

Born to Shop

This edition published by Ravette Publishing 2008.

ISBN: 978-1-84161-314-7

ℛℛ
RAVETTE PUBLISHING

Throw in the **trowel**, it's time for **tea**

Do **not** start with me, you will **not win**

Lawn
Enforcement
Officer

Gone
to
seed

Other BORN TO SHOP titles available ...

	ISBN	Price
All men are created equal... equally useless	978-1-84161-257-7	£4.9
Another day in paradise	978-1-84161-255-3	£4.9
Born to Shop non Stop	978-1-84161-283-6	£4.9
Friends are the family we choose for ourselves	978-1-84161-254-6	£4.9
I never met a calorie I didn't like	978-1-84161-256-0	£4.9
Life's too short to drink bad wine	978-1-84161-275-1	£4.9
M is Mother not for Maid	978-1-84161-274-4	£4.9
100% gorgeous ... most of the time	978-1-84161-284-3	£4.9

HOW TO ORDER   Please send a cheque/postal order in £ sterling, made payabl
to 'Ravette Publishing' for the cover price of the books and
allow the following for post & packaging ...

UK & BFPO	70p for the first book & 40p per book thereafter
Europe & Eire	£1.30 for the first book & 70p per book thereafter
Rest of the world	£2.20 for the first book & £1.10 per book thereafter

RAVETTE PUBLISHING LTD
Unit 3 Tristar Centre, Star Road, Partridge Green, West Sussex RH13 8RA
Tel: 01403 711443   Fax: 01403 711554   Email: ravettepub@aol.com

Prices and availability are subject to change without prior notice.